My Bird Journal

Terry Miller Shannon

Rigby®

A Harcourt Achieve Imprint

www.Rigby.com
1-800-531-5015

MARCH 16

Wow! Today I found something exciting right in my own backyard.

It was a nest in the fir tree near my house. I'm sure it's a bird's nest. Birds build nests so they'll have a safe place for laying eggs and raising families.

I wonder what kind of bird made this nest. Maybe there are eggs inside and if there are, I wonder if they will hatch.

I'm going to become a bird detective and find out. I'll keep notes just like real detectives. I'll need some tools to help me solve this mystery.

3

MARCH 17

This morning I talked to my dad about the things I'll need for my detective work. I told him a notebook was unnecessary, since I already had one. (It's the book I'm already writing in!) However, I'll need to borrow his **binoculars**. His binoculars are special because they also take pictures! My dad also gave me binoculars stickers that he bought, and I'm going to use them to label the pictures I take.

I wondered how I would be able to actually *see* inside the nest, but then Dad had an amazing idea. He suggested that I attach a mirror to a long pole. Then I can guide the mirror above the nest and peek inside! Dad says he will find a mirror and a pole, and then we'll make the tool together.

Things I Need

binoculars

notebook

pole

mirror

MARCH 18

Dad and I taped the mirror to the pole today. We used lots of thick, sturdy tape so that the mirror wouldn't fall off.

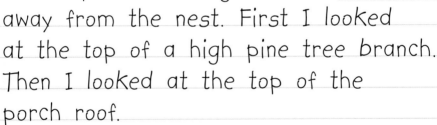

When I picked up my unusual tool, I realized it was uncomfortable and hard to use. I thought I should practice using it away from the nest. First I looked at the top of a high pine tree branch. Then I looked at the top of the porch roof.

Then my curiosity got the best of me! I stood away from the nest and slowly and carefully raised the mirror above it.

Wow! I could see inside the nest! My dad's idea worked! The nest was shaped like a cup. It looked like it was built out of twigs and was glued together with mud. It was lined with grass, too. The inside of the nest was about four inches across. I had my first clues!

Then I heard a bird singing nearby, but it seemed to be hiding. I wish I didn't have to go to school so I could watch the nest and solve the mystery!

MARCH 19

Here are some other things I know that may help me solve the bird nest mystery.

Clues:
* The time of the year is spring.
* I've seen these birds in the area around the nest: hummingbirds, quail, woodpeckers, and robins.
* I found a grayish-brown feather under the nest.

With Dad, I looked on the Internet to find out more about bird nests.

I looked up hummingbirds and discovered that their nests are about the size of a walnut. My nest seems to be too big for a hummingbird.

I read about woodpeckers, too. They make their nests in **cavities** in trees. I also learned that quail make their nests on the ground.

Finally I found something that seems to fit the description of the nest in our tree! The website described an American robin's nest as a cup-shaped nest of twigs and mud, lined with fine grass.

Woodpecker's nest

Quail's nest

Robin's nest

Hummingbird's nest

MARCH 20

I read more and more about robins and learned a lot of facts that I didn't know. For example, when robins build nests early in the spring, leaves haven't appeared on many trees. So at this time of year, they build in **evergreens**, like our fir tree, so their nests stay hidden. When they build nests in the summer, robins may build high in trees with leaves.

American Robin

The female robin chooses where the nest will be, and then the male robin helps the female build the nest. It takes a robin anywhere from two to six days to build a nest. The female robin shapes it with her beak, feet, and body.

Here's all I learned

Nests	Quail	Woodpecker	Hummingbird	Robin
Made in spring	yes	yes	yes	yes
Cup-shaped	no	no	yes	yes
Sits in tree branches	no	no	yes	yes
Four inches wide	no	sizes vary	no	yes

MARCH 21

This afternoon when I peeked carefully with my mirror, I saw one blue egg! How cool! Unfortunately, I had to leave to go to soccer practice, so I didn't get to watch the nest any longer.

Before I left for practice, though, I quickly looked at some bird books that I got at the library. I read that robins usually lay three to seven blue eggs.

I am quite the bird detective!

American Robin Egg

MARCH 21

This detective work sure is fun! Today there were two eggs in the nest! My bird book says a female robin will lay only one egg a day.

I pulled out the gray-brown feather I had found under the nest. According to the bird books, robins are mostly gray-brown with an orange or red chest.

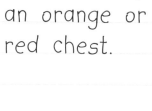

MARCH 23

There are three eggs in the nest today. One robin sat high in the tree and sang loudly while another one fluttered around on the other side of the yard. I knew they didn't want me near the nest, so I disappeared into the house. Instead I watched the nest from the window with my binoculars. I took this photo with the binoculars. It looks just like the photo I found on the Internet.

American Robin Eggs

Today I saw that there are still three eggs in the nest. I hadn't been watching for long when I saw a robin land on the

nest. It stayed there for a long time. When it left, another robin came and sat on the eggs to keep them warm.

This second robin had a blacker head and brighter feathers. My bird book says the brighter-colored bird is probably the father. I stayed far away from the nest so I wouldn't frighten the robins. I found a picture of a robin on the Internet that looks just like the one I saw today.

MARCH 25

This afternoon I read more about robins in my bird books. I discovered robin parents sit on their eggs for eleven to fourteen days to keep them warm so the chicks can develop inside. The grown robins protect the eggs from dangers, such as cats, raccoons, and other animals.

APRIL 6

I've been watching the robins sit on their eggs for two weeks now. They take turns keeping the eggs warm. My book says that robins sit on eggs for about forty minutes at a time. The mother bird turns the eggs gently with her beak to help keep them at the right temperature. Turning also helps keep the baby birds inside from sticking to the eggshells.

A mother bird will usually leave her eggs for only ten minutes or less. Sometimes the father robin **incubates** the eggs. He also stands guard and tries to get unwanted visitors (like me) to leave.

APRIL 7

Today I heard a "peep, peep, peep!" I found tiny pieces of blue eggshell on the ground below the nesl. I used the binoculars to look at the nest. I saw one scrawny, featherless baby bird with its beak wide open! It was red and wet. My bird books said baby birds are also blind when they're born.

Baby chick just hatched

Robin chick using its egg tooth to hatch

I read that the chicks should **hatch** one day apart, in the order the eggs were laid. I'm sure it's very hard work to hatch out of an egg. Each chick uses a hard hook that's on the end of its beak to break a hole in the eggshell. That hook is known as an egg tooth. It may take each chick an entire day to struggle out of its egg.

APRIL 8

Today there were two noisy baby birds in the nest. They wanted food, and they wanted it right away!

APRIL 9

This morning when I looked in the nest, there were three loud, hungry baby birds! The parents were really busy feeding their babies, finding more food, and watching over the nest. The parents also had to keep the nest clean by removing the babies' waste.

APRIL 10

Today I took a picture of a robin pulling an earthworm from our lawn. The adult robins feed their babies constantly, and the chicks keep begging for more food.

APRIL 25

Over the past two weeks, I noticed that the baby birds grew feathers. One by one, they left the nest, hopping out onto the branches before flying away.

I'm really sad because the nest is empty now and my detective work is over. I'd like to take the nest, but I'll leave it alone. My bird book said robins often return to the area they grew up in to build their own nests and lay eggs. The baby robins I've watched might someday come back to my yard to make nests, lay eggs, and raise their own families! I can't wait to see that!

Glossary

binoculars a double telescope made to be used with both eyes so faraway things look nearer and larger

cavities holes

evergreens trees that stay green all year

hatch to break out of an egg

incubates keeps something warm so it will grow

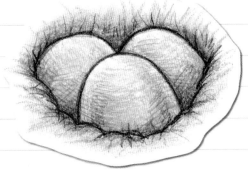